SIGNALS FROM THE ATLANTIC CABLE.

AN ADDRESS,

BY C. VAN RENSSELAER.

C. SHERMAN & SON, PRINTERS.

THE

PRESBYTERIAN

HISTORICAL ALMANAC,

AND

Annual Remembrancer of the Church,

FOR 1858-9.

COMPILED AND ARRANGED BY

Joseph M. Wilson.

OUR PROPOSITION

Is to supply a want often felt and expressed by our Ministers and Elders, by publishing in a convenient form a volume containing all the details and operations of THE PRESBYTERIAN CHURCH during the year ending with the Annual Sessions of 1858.

We will here remark that we use the word Presbyterian in its widest and most comprehensive sense, viz: To include all branches known as Presbyterian—in the United States, British Provinces, Great Britain and Ireland.

As we deem this, the most direct way of calling attention to the volume, we give a brief synopsis of its Contents.

The work will contain a *Calendar* showing events of interest to Presbyterians, Ecclesiastical and Historical, to correspond with the days of each month, arranged with care, by a Literary gentleman of this city [Philadelphia].

The Opening of the Seventieth Session of THE GENERAL ASSEMBLY OF THE PRESBYTERIAN CHURCH in the First Presbyterian Church, New Orleans, La., on Thursday the 6th of May, 1858, by Rev. CORTLANDT VAN RENSSELAER, D. D., Moderator of the last Assembly, with an outline of his discourse.

A List of the Members of the Assembly, arranged alphabetically, with the names of the Presbyteries and Synods which they represented.

The Election of the Moderator, Rev. WILLIAM A. SCOTT, D. D., of San Francisco—with a fine *Portrait* engraved expressly for this Almanac, by NEWSAM.

The Acts and Resolutions passed by the General Assembly, viz:

The Bills and Overtures, The Judicial Cases, The Synodical Reports, and Miscellaneous Resolutions offered—with the action of the Assembly.

The Narrative of the State of Religion, to which will be appended a *Table*, showing the names of Ministers who have died during the year, their Presbytery, the year of their Ordination, their death, their age, and the disease which closed their life.

A full and complete exposition of the Annual Reports of the Boards and Committees connected with the Church; also, the Theological Seminaries,

Colleges, Academies, Parochial Schools, &c., their financial operations, and such comparative tables as will enable the reader to form a just estimate of their progress and extent of the work.

A list of the Moderators of the General Assembly since its organization, with the name of the Presbytery to which they belonged when elected, the year of their ordination, death and age, the place of meeting.

A list of the Ministers and Licentiates, alphabetically arranged, with an Initial Letter, indicating their position, whether pastor, stated supply, &c. Also, the name of the Presbytery to which they belong, and their Post offices, corrected up to the time of going to press.

Synodical and Presbyterial Tables, with several additional columns, arranged alphabetically; the name of stated Clerk; the number of Presbyteries, Ministers, Communicants, &c. &c., divided into two tables, one called the Personal, the other the Financial Statistics of the Church.

A Historical Sketch of the FIRST PRESBYTERIAN CHURCH, N. Orleans, La., where the Assembly held its session, by Rev. B. M. PALMER, D. D., Pastor, with a *fine view of the building.*

The Opening of the Sixty-fourth Session of THE GENERAL ASSEMBLY OF THE PRESBYTERIAN CHURCH, in the Second Presbyterian Church, Chicago, Illinois, on Thursday, May 20th, 1858, by Rev. SAMUEL W. FISHER, D. D., Moderator of the last Assembly, with an outline of his discourse.

A List of the Members of the Assembly, alphabetically arranged, with the names of the Presbyteries and Synods they represented.

The Election of Rev. M. L. P. THOMPSON, D. D., of Buffalo, N. Y., Moderator, with a fine *Portrait,* by Newsam.

The Acts and Resolutions adopted by the Assembly.

A Narrative of the State of Religion, to which will be added a list of the Ministers who have died during the year, arranged in a table, showing their name, Presbytery, ordination, death, age and disease.

A clear and well-arranged abstract of the Annual Reports of *The Permanent Committees* of the General Assembly.

A list of the Moderators since the organization of the General Assembly.

Synodical and Presbyterial Tables, arranged alphabetically, with the usual amount of statistical matter, together with several additional columns.

A complete list of the Ministers and Licentiates, alphabetically arranged, with their Presbyteries and Post-offices.

A History of the SECOND PRESBYTERIAN CHURCH IN CHICAGO, in which the Assembly held its session, by Rev. Dr. PATTERSON, Pastor, together with a finely engraved *view of the building.*

The History of the UNITED SYNOD OF THE PRESBYTERIAN CHURCH IN THE UNITED STATES, with all the Papers and Documents concerning its origin and organization. Prepared by Rev. CHAS. H. READ, D. D., of Richmond, Va.

The opening of the First Session of the United Synod of the PRESBYTERIAN CHURCH, in the Second Presbyterian Church, Knoxville, Tenn., on the 2nd of April, 1858, by Rev. J. D. MITCHELL, D. D., with an outline of his discourse.

The List of Members of the Synod, (arranged as the others).

The Election of Rev. CHAS. H. READ, D. D., Moderator, with a fine PORTRAIT by *Newsam.*

The Acts and Resolutions passed. The Presbyterial and Synodical Tables.

The List of Ministers and Licentiates, with Presbytery and Post-offices.

A History of the SECOND PRESBYTERIAN CHURCH, Knoxville, Tennessee, where the Synod held its first Session, by Rev. JOSEPH H. MARTIN, Pastor, with a fine view of the Church Building.

The Opening of the Fifty-seventh Session of the ASSOCIATE SYNOD of North America, in the First Associate Presbyterian Church, Pittsburg, Pa., May 19th, 1858, by Rev. DAVID W. FRENCH, *Moderator* of the last Synod, with an outline of his discourse.
The List of the Members of the Synod, (arranged as the others).
The Election of the Moderator, Rev. JOSEPH T. COOPER, D. D., of Philadelphia, with a fine Portrait, by *Newsam*.
The Acts and Resolutions passed during the Session.
The Presbyterial and Synodical Tables; A List of Members and Licentiates arranged with the Presbytery and Post-offices.
A *History of the First Associate Presbyterian Church, Pittsburgh, Pa.*, by Rev. SAM'L B. REED, Pastor, where the Synod held its last session, and a FINE VIEW of the building.

The Opening of the Annual Meeting of the General Synod of the *Associate Reformed Presbyterian Church*, in the First A. R. Church, Allegheny City, Pa., the 19th of May 1858, by Rev. D. R. KERR, D.D., with an outline of his Discourse.
A List of Members of Synod (arranged as the others.)
The Election of the Moderator, Rev. D. C. McLAREN, D. D., of Geneva, N.Y., with a fine Portrait.
The Acts and Resolutions passed. The usual Presbyterial Tables.
The List of Ministers and Licentiates, with Presbyteries and Post-office.
An Historical Sketch of the *First Associate Reformed Presbyterian Church*, by Rev. JOHN T. PRESSLY, D.D., with a *fine view of the building.*

The Organization of THE UNITED PRESBYTERIAN CHURCH, with the details connected with this important event—with a fine Portrait of Rev. JOHN T. PRESSLY, D. D., the first Moderator.

The thirty-fifth Session of the General Synod of the REFORMED PRESBYTERIAN CHURCH IN NORTH AMERICA, was held in the First Reformed Presbyterian Church, Eden, Illinois, May 27, 1858, and was opened by Rev. J. AGNEW CRAWFORD, Moderator of last year, with an outline of his Discourse.
—The members of the Synod (arranged as the others.)
The Election of the Moderator, Rev. ANDREW GIFFORD WYLIE, of Duanesburgh, N.Y., with a fine PORTRAIT by *Newsam*.
The Acts and Resolutions passed by Synod. The Presbyterial Tables, &c.
The List of Ministers, with Presbytery and Post-office.
A Historical Sketch of the First Reformed Presbyterian Church, Eden, Ill., by Rev. SAM'L WYLIE, Pastor, with a FINE VIEW OF THE CHURCH.

The opening of the twenty eighth session of the General Assembly of the *Cumberland Presbyterian Church*, in the Presbyterian Church, Huntsville, Alabama, on Thursday, May 20th, 1858, by Rev. C. P. REED, with an outline of his Discourse.
A List of the Members of the Assembly, (arranged as the others.)
The Election of Rev. FELIX JOHNSON, D. D., of Lagrange, Ala., Moderator, with a *Portrait*.
The Acts and Resolutions passed, &c. &c. The Synodical Tables, &c. &c.
A List of the Ministers, arranged with Presbytery and Post-office.

The Meeting of the ASSOCIATE REFORMED SYNOD OF THE SOUTH; held in Old Providence Church, Augusta county, Virginia, Oct. 12th, 1857, was opened with a discourse from Rev. D. G. PHILLIPS.

A List of the members of Synod, (arranged as the others.)

The Acts and Resolutions passed and the Presbyterial Reports.

A List of Ministers, &c.

The REFORMED PRESBYTERIAN CHURCH in North America, met in Northwood, Ohio, May 1857, and was opened with a Discourse by the Moderator, (this body did not meet in 1858.) We give a list of its Ministers, &c.

A Sketch or the *Presbyterian Historical Society*. Also a large number of matters of general interest.

BRITISH PROVINCES.

The meeting of the *Presbyterian Church of Canada*, was held in the McNab Street Presbyterian Church, Hamilton, C. W. A Synopsis of the Proceedings and such details as come within the design of this work. The Election of Moderator, Rev. THOS WARDROPE, of Ottawa, C. W., with a fine *Portrait.*

An Historical Sketch of the McNab Street Presbyterian Church, Hamilton, by Rev. D. INGLIS, Pastor, and a *fine view of the building.*

We will give an account of the various Presbyterian bodies in Canada West, Nova Scotia, Prince Edward Island, New Brunswick, the names of Ministers, with Presbytery and Post-office—but, the limits of this circular prevents a full detail.

GREAT BRITAIN AND IRELAND.

The Meeting of the Irish General Assembly in the Presbyterian Church, Londonderry. The Election of Rev. JOHN JOHNSTON, of Banbridge, Ireland, Moderator, with a fine *Portrait.* Also a full account of the proceedings.

An Historical Sketch of the Church, Londonderry, by Rev. WM. CLURE, Pastor, and a *fine view of the building,* including *Walker's Monument.*

An account of the Free Church of Scotland. The Presbyterian Church of Scotland; the various Synods—English and Scotch.

☞ We would call attention to the fact that the *Portraits* are all from Daguerreotypes or Ambrotypes taken expressly for the Almanac, and are by an artist who is one of the best in the country; they are crayon lithographs.

The *views of the Churches* are also new and prepared from drawings for this Almanac. *The Publisher* hopes this effort will be sustained, as from the character of the volume its sale is limited to *the Presbyterians.*

The *Historical Almanac* will be a large octavo volume, printed on good paper. Price will be $1.00 sent by mail, free of postage. As it is necessary to know the size of the Edition to print, those wishing copies will send their *names* as early as possible. Address,

JOSEPH M. WILSON, Publisher,

No. 111 South Tenth St., below Chesnut,

PHILADELPHIA.

P. S. The Publisher will also receive, to be published with the Almanac, *Advertisements* for Schools, Academies, Colleges, Books, Insurance Companies, &c. &c. Those wishing to advertise will please apply immediately. The work will be issued the latter part of October, 1858.

Signals from the Atlantic Cable.

AN ADDRESS

DELIVERED AT

THE TELEGRAPHIC CELEBRATION,

SEPTEMBER 1st, 1858,

IN THE CITY HALL, BURLINGTON, NEW JERSEY.

BY

CORTLANDT VAN RENSSELAER.

PHILADELPHIA:
JOSEPH M. WILSON, PUBLISHER,
NO. 111 SOUTH TENTH STREET.
1858.

BURLINGTON CELEBRATION.

THE Celebration of the successful laying of the ATLANTIC CABLE took place in Burlington, N. J., on September 1st, 1858, according to the following Programme, issued by the Committee of Arrangements:

"ATLANTIC CABLE CELEBRATION.

"REV. C. VAN RENSSELAER, D. D.

"DEAR SIR: We live in an age of astonishing events. This nineteenth century has been more marked than any that has preceded it by the triumphs of mind over matter; and the greatest of them all has just been accomplished, in the successful laying of the Telegraph Cable, which unites the Old World with the New. On Wednesday, the 1st proximo, an immense number of the people of the United States will be engaged in celebrating this most marvellous event, by public parades, the firing of artillery, fireworks, and other demonstrations of joy. Perhaps it may be more in character for our quiet people to adopt a somewhat different method of joining in the general rejoicing.

"The undersigned, on behalf of a number of their fellow-citizens, respectfully request you to deliver an Address upon this magnificent achievement, on the evening of said day, at 7½ o'clock, at the City Hall. If you are willing to comply with this request, you will greatly oblige many of your friends.

"Respectfully, your friends,
"SAMUEL R. GUMMERE,
"SAMUEL KEYS,
"J. HOWARD PUGH.

"BURLINGTON, Aug. 30, 1858.

"TO MESSRS. SAMUEL R. GUMMERE, SAMUEL KEYS, AND J. HOWARD PUGH.

"GENTLEMEN: There seems to be a propriety in our uniting with other cities in the celebration of the event which brings two hemispheres into telegraphic communication. I will endeavour to prepare an Address suitable to the occasion; and I trust that you will accept my sincere desire to draw the proper lessons from this great achievement as an excuse for any deficiencies resulting from hasty preparation, or any other cause.

"I am yours, respectfully,
"C. VAN RENSSELAER.

"In accordance with the above correspondence, the undersigned respectfully invite the ladies and gentlemen of the City of Burlington and its vicinity, to assemble at the CITY HALL, on WEDNESDAY, September 1st, at 7½ o'clock P. M., to hear an address appropriate to the occasion by the REV. C. VAN RENSSELAER.

"A Band of Music will be in attendance.

"The Bells of the City will be rung on Wednesday from 12 to 1 P. M.

"Samuel R. Gummere, Samuel Keys, J. Howard Pugh, James Watts, Nathan Harper, Joseph E. Taylor, Charles G. Milnor, John B. Roberts, Samuel J. Gummere, John Rodgers.—*Committee of Citizens.*

"BURLINGTON, N. J., August 31, 1858."

EXERCISES AT THE CITY HALL.

The City Hall was crowded, at the appointed time, by an intelligent audience, numbers being unable to gain admittance. Samuel R. Gummere was called to the Chair; and briefly addressed the people. After which, the following was the order of exercises.

1. "Hail Columbia," by the Burlington Band.

2. An Introductory, written by request, by a young Lady, residing in Burlington, which is here inserted. Read by Mr. Gummere.

Give thanks! give thanks, and pause awhile,
In view of this last glorious gift of Heaven;
And humbly bend, and worship Him, who made
Man of such wondrous, self-amazing powers!
Time is, yet is not! Distance stands,
Yet parts, no longer, man from fellow-man!
Thought, flying on electric chain, across
The deep, dark Ocean, now can find response
Immediate! God, in mercy, deigns
To give to man another wondrous power:
And places in his hand that lightning pen
With which, He, even, sometime deigned to write,
To warn of danger, or to summon quick
To His dread audience! Let us bow
In awe, and take the blessing given,
Remembering 'tis from His great presence come;
And as it works subservient to our will,
Oh! let us trembling strive to work His own.

3. Prayer by the Rev. Mr. Lewis, of the Methodist Church.

4. "God save the Queen," by the Band.

5. Address by the Rev. C. Van Rensselaer, D. D.

6. "The Star-Spangled Banner" and the "Marseillaise," by the Band.

7. Mrs. Ann S. Stephens's Ode, written for the Celebration in New York, and sung, at the request of the audience, by Mr. Haas.

8. "Rule Britannia," by the Band.

On motion of Captain H. McDowell, of the Marion Rifle Corps (who were present in their uniform) it was

"Resolved, That the thanks of this meeting be tendered to the Rev. Dr. Van Rensselaer for his address on this interesting occasion, and that the Committee of Arrangements be authorized to request a copy for publication."

9. "Yankee Doodle," by the Band.

10. The Benediction, by the Rev. Mr. Meason, of the Baptist Church.

The meeting broke up with much apparent satisfaction; and Burlington thus endeavoured to contribute its share in the commemoration of one of the most important events of the nineteenth century.

ADDRESS.

My Fellow-citizens of Burlington:
Ladies and Gentlemen.

The union of the two hemispheres is a festival event in the history of the great globe. America, from Greenland to Magellan, thrills with continental joy at the pressure of the sister hands of Europe, Asia, and Africa. And the mighty hemisphere of the East, in one family three, receives, with kindred emotion, the welcome grasp of a long-separated and absent member of the terrestrial household.

The globe is now in electric union. Ye winds, who have swept over American forests, and African deserts, and Asiatic mountains, and European plains, a new agent, swifter far than your aerial speed, is a visitant of the four quarters of the globe. Ye stars of light, who chronicle new achievements in the infinite universe, record in the book of ages the laying of the thought-wire that speaks to nations through separating gulfs. Ye mountains, sublime in the peaks of everlasting hills, let your primeval rocks and verdure respond to the human enterprise which has mounted your Alpine heights, and has now thrown the rein of mastery over your submerged depths, and guides its way across the rugged mountain-path of waters. And thou, old ocean, majestic in the billows of thy might, that anthem the praise of God from shore to shore,—thou, who leadest the intercourse of nations by outspreading sail and grander steam, to thine azure deep is committed a new trained elemental power, from the hands of Him who rules the waves and directs the storm.

The air, the sky, the earth, the sea, send greeting to the festival of men, and make one with the nations, in their simultaneous celebration, of an influential and great event in the history of the nineteenth century.

Occasions like the present have their high moral purposes. They serve to explain and illustrate the discovery they celebrate; they magnify to its true proportions the triumph of mind over matter; they secure to society an interval of intellectual and genial festivity; they exert an elevating and educating influence on the popular mind; they render homage to providential developments in the world's affairs; and they assist in bringing God to view as the great and glorious Ruler of the Universe.

Fellow-citizens of Burlington, it is becoming to the dignity of this ancient city, and to its educational and industrial spirit, to unite with other cities in this and in distant lands, in celebrating the successful laying of the ATLANTIC TELEGRAPH. This is one of those leading and happy events in human history, which, when it occurs first, anticipates the emotions and honours of future triumphs of the same kind. Now is the time and the hour! Our celebration, on the appointed day, brings us into heartfelt connection with the general joy and praise; and the telegraphic poles of Burlington exchange signals with the wires on Albion's cliffs, and return the festival flashes, which pulse with the power of life, from our commercial metropolis to the outstretched boundaries of this great Republic.

The subject of our meditations shall be SOME OF THE LESSONS TAUGHT BY THE LAYING OF THE ATLANTIC TELEGRAPH. If I have succeeded in reading any of them, I desire to signal to you their true import, and to stand for a few minutes in sympathetic, electric union with your minds and hearts,—an operator to explain some of the signs and the seasons in the horizon of the awe-struck world.

I. The first lesson of the submerged telegraph is clearly THE SUPERINTENDENCE OF DIVINE PROVIDENCE IN THE AFFAIRS OF MEN. The time and the issuing of this event proclaim the hand of God. Occurring a century, or half a century ago, it would have been incongruous to human affairs. The world was not in a condition to appreciate or profit by an invention which antedated its necessity. God arranges all things so that everything shall be in its place, at the right time, in the mighty system of his advancing Providence. The clock on the dial of ages strikes, only when the seconds and minutes make up the hour. As the discovery of America was not demanded by the condition of the world, prior to the bold and hopeful adventure of the divinely guided Columbus, so an oceanic telegraph came into being only when the wants of the nineteenth century sought it out among the ordained inventions of a responsive Providence. The discovery of America in 1492 stands related to the counsels of God, just as the laying of the Atlantic telegraph in 1858. God is in history. Divinity overshadows every event with grandeur, and gives to it, like the stars, its right ascension in a sphere of glory.

The successful issue of the event we celebrate, as well as its time, brings to view divine Providence. Man walks beyond the bounds of his domain, when he undertakes to thread over, by the line of his skill, mountain peaks, submerged in ocean's depths. Adventurous was he, who first unfurled a sail upon the billows of the defiant deep; but what language can express the boldness, and even hopelessness of that enterprise that seeks to conquer, not space on the surface wave, but on the unexplored mud and cavern in the darkness of the distant bottom? To what but the interposing help of divine Providence can be ascribed the successful deposit, in the lower parts of the boisterous ocean, of a wire, measured in size by a human finger and in length by a twelfth part of the distance around the globe?

In 1857, the first Atlantic experiment was made. On the 5th of August of that year, two ships, well named—the "Agamemnon," after an indomitable Greek chieftain, and thus representing the spirit of men; the "Niagara," after the great cataract, and representing the wonders of nature—these two vessels set sail with the mysterious cable, one end of which is held by the Old World, as the pledge of its firm faith in the enterprise. Five days out from land, on the 11th of August, the slender cord, intended to reach the New World, is broken by the heaving of the vessel; and the part submerged, of three hundred and forty-four miles, is left a buried and irrecoverable fragment amid the curves of the Atlantic plateau. Thus perished the hopes of the first expedition. Man's ability was inadequate to the work.

On the 10th of June, 1858, the undaunted ships again set out. Violent storms forebode disaster. The Agamemnon is shaken to and fro by the sea, as if to exult over the frailty of human workmanship, and the vessel barely escapes wreck. At last the cable is joined in mid-ocean, and the ships part for the two hemispheres. On the first day the wire is broken on the Niagara, on the second day at the bottom of the ocean, and on the fourth day on the Agamemnon. Three failures, with the loss of three hundred and thirty-five miles of cable, again rebuke human impotency. The Niagara returns in gloom, followed by her cheerless but not discomfited compeer. The conviction settles on the popular mind that the enterprise is beyond human power. And so it is. But not beyond God's. The Lord on high is mightier than the waves of the sea.

On the third expedition the noble ships reached their mid-ocean rendezvous on the 27th of July, true to each other as the needle to the pole, and eager to make the magnet available at the bottom of the ocean as on its surface. The splice was effectually, but this time rudely made; and "the apparatus was then dropped into the sea without any formality, and indeed almost without a spectator; for those on board the ship had witnessed so many beginnings to the telegraphic line, that it was evident they despaired of there ever being an end to it." The fact is, that public opinion, both on sea and land, had reached such a point of depression and of renunciation of human ability, as to produce the general feeling that, without the special interposition of Providence, the work must prove a failure. Thus did God prepare the world to put its trust in Him alone. Where else is trust safe?

The ships now slowly part from each other in the concealed glory of a successful mission. Painful anxiety keeps watch on both vessels. The pilots scan the sea rather than the stars, and the interest is at the stern and not at the prow. Never did maternal affection note, with more tenderness, the breathings of a new-born infant, than did the electricians the continuity of life developed by this wonderful child of nature in the cradle of the deep. Day after day passes without disaster; but, like the crisis between life and death, apprehension only increases until complete safety is announced. The logs of both ships show the variety of contingencies which alternately cherished or depressed hope. The story of the double passage reads, indeed, like the romance of the adventures in the earlier voyages of discovery. But here is the higher moral sublimity of a great and well-matured enterprise, throwing its lights and shadows over the scene. What dangers encompass the daring work! Behold the little line, sparkling by day in the sunbeams, and in the night leaving its slight, phosphorescent track of foam, like silver, on the billows. Is it to reach, at last, its twofold destination? What perils of wind and storm, of waves, and icebergs, and whales, has it to encounter! What perils of Yankee vessels dashing up with unapologizing curiosity to spy out the mystery of the strange proceedings! What perils from the uncoiling of the spiral heaps of those miles of wire; from splicing and running out from one part of the ship to another; from the standing still, as on one occasion on the Agamemnon, of the paying-out wheels of the machinery, when the vast ship hung on to the frail cord; above all, what perils from crossing the unknown heights and valleys of the sea, unvisited by man, save by a few plunges of his long sounding-line, or by his own lifeless frame asleep in the watery sepulchre! Columbus on the prow of the Santa Maria, in search of the New World, depicts the double gaze, easterly and westerly, of the eager hearts on the Agamemnon and Niagara. The water at length shallows; the sounding-line telegraphs approaching land; the two harbours are won, and God is glorified.

On the 5th of August, the cable is landed on both shores. The Niagara's portion is carried up in glad but toiling procession to the station-house; and the end being placed in connection with the instrument, the deflection of the needle on the galvanometer shows a good electrical condition in the cable. And then and there, in the silence of the awe inspired by success from heaven, and amid the rude scenes of the station-house in the wilderness, the good Captain Hudson, assembling his men, *remembers God* and PRAYS. Few of earth's scenes were more sublime than that one, in the forests of Newfoundland. It stands out in the foreground of history, like Columbus kneeling before God on the soil of the New World, or De Soto planting the cross on the banks of the Mississippi, or Brewster and the Pilgrims praying and singing psalms at the landing-Rock of Plymouth. Let this scene go down to posterity among the grandest memorials of our national history!

The religious services were introduced by a few appropriate words, beginning with these: "The work has been performed, not by ourselves: there has been an Almighty hand over us and aiding us; and without the divine assistance, thus extended, success was impossible." In the same spirit of "glory to God in the highest," Captain Hudson sent his first telegraphic announcement in the memorable words, "GOD HAS BEEN WITH US. THE TELEGRAPHIC CABLE IS LAID, WITHOUT ACCIDENT; AND TO HIM BE ALL THE GLORY."

This great truth, then, of *God's holy Providence in the world's affairs*, is flashed from Valentia to Trinity Bay, from Europe to America, and around the circuit of the globe, up into the bright arches of the eternal heavens.

II. Another of the lessons, signalled by the Atlantic Telegraph, is THE TRIUMPH OF HUMAN GENIUS, FAITH, AND PERSEVERANCE.

Let it be distinctly acknowledged that every endowment of man is from God. It is the inspiration of the Almighty that giveth understanding. The triumphs of man's intellect are his own, only as the *aided* emanations of a created *instrumentality*.

The human mind, like the stars which differ in glory, has its variations of capacity. The masses are scarcely perceptible on the map of the firmament, inferior glimmerings, or nebulæ undistinguishable in the vast abyss of being. The morning and the evening star is solitary in the grandeur of its brightness. Superior intellects are rare; but with what power they attract and rule! Great men in science and the arts, whose inventions and discoveries advance civilization, reign to distant ages.

Man's intellect, however, is comparatively feeble in its best estate. The children of a succeeding generation often know more than was at first discerned by the mind of inventive genius. Three considerations modify, without disowning, the homage due to the triumphs of the human mind. *First*, new discoveries and inventions generally originate from small and suggestive incidents, and not from independent, original investigation. Thus, the falling of an apple suggested to Newton's mind the principle of gravitation. The idea of the *telescope* grew out of the experiment of a boy, who, in using two lenses, found that a church-steeple was brought nearer in an inverted form. The properties of the *magnetic needle* were discovered by "some curious persons who were amusing themselves by floating a loadstone, suspended upon a piece of cork, in a basin of water, which, when left at liberty, was observed to point to the north." The *art of printing* derived its origin from the effort of a man in Haarlem to amuse his children by transferring to paper some letters he had cut on the smooth bark of a tree. A new epoch was created in the department of *galvanism*, or *animal electricity*, by Madame Galvani's notice of the convulsions in the muscles of frogs by the contact of metals. Electricity for telegraphic purposes was first stumbled upon by Oersted, of Copenhagen, who observed that an electric current, transmitted through a wire placed parallel to a magnetic needle, either above or below it, caused the needle to deviate to the right or left, according to the direction of the current. In short, the triumphs of genius in the arts and sciences generally owe their origin to suggestive and casual incidents, and not to the original determinations of the human intellect.

Secondly. Discoveries and inventions are *the work of more than one mind.* Not to multiply illustrations, let us take the single subject of Electricity, the great agent in telegraphing. Dr. Gilbert, of Colchester, is the first to record, in 1660, the phenomenon of electricity, which he produced from various substances. Seven years later, Otto Guericke, of Germany, brought out the electric machine, now so common, although still an object of wonder. In 1730, Stephen Grey divided all material substances into electrics and non-electrics; and shortly after, Dufaye discovered the phenomena of attraction and repulsion. The experiments of Kleist, Cunœus, and Muschenbrœk, dating from 1746, led to the discovery of the Leyden jar in 1755. About this time, Franklin proved by his little kite the identity between electricity and lightning, and gave a new impulse to the science, by establishing the universality of the fluid in nature. About 1780, Cavendish laid the foundation of chemical electricity, by decomposing air and water by means of this agent. In 1790 Galvani, and in 1800 Volta, added to the advances of this science by the discoveries of animal magnetism and the construction of the Voltaic battery. And in 1819, Oersted announced the discovery of Electro-Magnetism, or the relations between Electricity and Magnetism, which constitutes the basis of the telegraphic art. These successive developments of this particular science serve to show that, however great are the successes of intellect, no one mind can ever lay open the treasures of even a single vein in the strata of knowledge.

In the *third* place, it requires time to bring all discoveries into practical use. Even after the leading principle has been discovered, the human mind is slow in applying it to its practical ends. The power of steam was long known; but it was not until 1765 that Watt's invention of performing condensation in a separate vessel from the cylinder was applied to the steam engine; and still more notable, it was not until 1807, or nearly half a century later, that Fulton succeeded in propelling a steamboat on the Hudson River; and not until 1830 that steam was successfully applied to railways.

The Electro-Magnetic Telegraph, like the Steam Engine and other inventions, is the creature of gradual development. Oersted in 1819 discovered the principle of electro-magnetic power; and in 1820, the celebrated Ampère proposed to apply the principle to a telegraph, with the crude suggestion that as many magnetic needles and as many circuits should be employed as there were characters to be indicated. Schelling and Fechner proposed the employment of fewer needles. *Gauss* demonstrated, afterwards, that the appropriate combination of a few simple signs was all that was necessary to form a language for telegraphic purposes. *Sturgeon*, of England, was the first to construct an electro-magnet by coiling a copper wire around an iron of horseshoe shape. *Barlow*, of England, in 1825, failed to render his telegraph available, on account of the rapid diminution of the galvanic action with the distance, under the arrangements which he made. The great *desideratum* was to propel the galvanic power through an indefinite circuit of wire. In 1831, Professor *Joseph Henry*, now Secretary of the Smithsonian Institution, showed by his experiments how enormously more powerful magnets might be constructed, while the battery remained the same; and he also showed *how* and *why* the battery might be so arranged that the rapid diminution of the effect of galvanism might be prevented, so that *the effect could be produced in sufficient intensity at a great distance;* that is, so that we might TELEGRAPH. Professor Henry's discovery attracted much attention in the scientific world; but he did not himself undertake to invent a machine for telegraphing, or to decipher the language of electro-magnetism. In 1833, *Weber*, of Gottingen, found that a wire for telegraphic purposes on land required no special insulation; and in this year, in connection with *Gauss*, set in operation a telegraph between the Observatory of Gottingen and the Cabinet of Natural Philosophy, by means of a wire a mile and a half long. In 1835, Professor *Morse*, of New York, constructed in the University of New York, an electro-magnetic Telegraph, about a third of a mile long, and transmitted the word "Eureka" to paper. In 1837 much progress was made. In June of that year, *Cook* and *Wheatstone*, of England, took out their patent, using a deflective point; in July, *Steinheil* constructed a telegraph between Munich and Bogenhausen, employing a deflected needle to make dots and marks, as representatives of the alphabet; and in October of the same year, Professor *Morse* filed his caveat, which gave a general outline of his present system. In this paper, Professor Morse dates his inventions back to 1832, the year following Professor Henry's discoveries; but telegraphing, under his superintendence did not go into practical use on a large scale, until the completion of the Washington and Baltimore line in 1844. At first, two wires were considered necessary to make the circuit, one at the terminus and the other back. *Steinheil*, however, discovered that one-half of the circuit could be formed by the earth, and that double wires were unnecessary.

In the matter of veritable telegraphing, in the present acceptation of that word, Professor Morse, of New York, is justly entitled to pre-eminence among all the inventors of instruments that applied the previously discovered principles. So many minds have, in fact, co-operated to produce the telegraph to its present working order, that it may be called the invention of the age, rather than of any individual. Nevertheless, Professor Morse, more than any one man, has the credit of bringing the telegraph into practical use on a large scale; sustaining to the telegraph the same relation that Fulton does to steam navigation.*

Even after the operations of the telegraph were successful on land, it was a bold thought to drop the wire into the bed of the ocean for international communication. But time assists the triumphs of genius and perseverance. In November, 1851, the submarine telegraph was laid between Dover and Calais, a distance of 23½ miles; and on the same day guns were fired at Dover by means of the electric spark, communicated from Calais. Franklin had, however, anticipated the experiment in another mode, and had fired spirits by an electric current over a river, a century before, in 1748. Planting his Leyden jar, or battery, on one side of the Schuylkill, the philosopher, as an electro-King, commanded the electric current to the other side on a wire, and then summoned it to return by way of the river and earth. Perhaps, before long, some Yankee hand, fond of exploits, may apply American electricity, through the Atlantic ocean, to the touch-hole of British cannon, to astonish the Royal Lion and the Londoners. Various submarine telegraphs have been set in operation since 1851; but the greatest of all is the ATLANTIC TELEGRAPH OF 1858.

It does not detract from this great submarine work, that so many instrumentalities were necessary to its execution. Almost every philosopher has made some contribution to the elucidation of its scientific principles, especially Oersted, Gauss, Sturgeon, Henry, Weber, Steinheil, and Wheatstone; almost every inventor has aided in bringing it into practical use, especially Gauss, Weber, Wheatstone, Morse, and Steinheil; hundreds have assisted in laying the Atlantic cable—Brooke and Berryman in sounding and surveying the ocean path; Maury in foretelling the time of genial skies; Armstrong in applying gutta percha as the insulating material; Field in organizing the companies, furnishing the means, and superintending the whole work; the manufacturers, Glass and Elliott, and Newell, whose cunning skill wrought the ingenious wires; Berdan and Everett, who invented the paying-out machinery; Woodhouse and Canning, the engineers; Bright and Whitehouse, the electricians; Preely and Hudson, Dayman and Oldham, the commanders; Morse and Bache in their constant and valuable counsel from beginning to end; the British and American governments, who supplied the vessels; the gallant tars and laborious

* In this brief sketch of the discoveries and inventions relating to the Telegraph—which has been compiled from the various sources accessible to the public—the *intention* has been to be impartial, and to give to each individual his due share of honour.

working-men, who encountered toil day and night;—but, whatever number of persons may have been employed, intellectually or physically, in laying the Atlantic cable, it is certain that the work done is a great work, and that the mind of man, which fathomed the idea and anchored it in the deep, has a mighty range for its exploits, even from the stars of heaven down to the chambers of ocean's darkness.

Whilst due honour should be awarded to all, on both sides of the Atlantic, who have aided, by thought or hand, this transmarine achievement, the names that will be forever most dear to American minds are FRANKLIN, HENRY, MORSE, and FIELD:—*Franklin*, for identifying lightning with electricity, and thus connecting earth with the heavens; *Henry*, for devising the means and demonstrating the practicability of telegraphing through an indefinitely long circuit of wire; *Morse*, for reducing the electric current to a written language; and *Field*, for successfully executing the great sub-Atlantic enterprise.

The present commemoration holds in special honour the *laying of the Atlantic cable.* This work involved three separate and special classes of difficulties:—1. The organization of the men and means for the enterprise, including the immense cost of the experiment, which was about two millions of dollars. 2. The making of the right kind of cable, which involved the greatest skill in the selection of materials and in their mechanical combination into one cord. 3. The laying of the line at the bottom of the ocean, which required the space of two large vessels, careful coiling and uncoiling, and paying out into the sea by the most ingenious machinery.

The present celebration gives mingled homage to science, art, and practical skill. Taken all together, the combinations of the Atlantic Telegraph constitute unquestionably one of the greatest triumphs ever accomplished by the human intellect. The event teaches a lesson of faith, energy, and perseverance, to universal man.

III. Another lesson of the Atlantic Telegraph is that IT BRINGS GREAT ADVANTAGES, political, social, economical, and religious, to the world. Many benefits, numerous as its own seven-fold cord, are wrapped up in the inventory of those mysterious strands.

1. The promotion of the *friendship of nations* is one of the first natural advantages of the Atlantic Telegraph. The division of the world into different nations by means of mountains, rivers, and oceans, is a part of the arrangements of infinite goodness. Great ends of mercy, as well as of retribution, were answered by the confusion of tongues and the dispersion of mankind. In the progress of ages, the diversity, necessary to the best interests of the race, was to be relieved by the providential preparations for a more genial intercourse. The sharp, repulsive prejudices and rude hostilities of the earlier eras of civilization were to be superseded by a system of attracting influences. At the present day all the ten-

dencies of the world's advancement are towards intercourse, unity, and peace. The swift communication of thought is the best harbinger of universal concord. As the original dispersion of mankind was accomplished by the confusion of language at the tower of Babel, so its reunion in the bonds of peace is promoted by the creation of a new, universal language, outstripping the resources of combined human tongues.

The wire itself symbolizes the union of all lands, and the fraternity, which Grace is to give to the nations. Higher than physical juxtaposition is the intellectual and moral nearness of vision that outstrips the course of the sun, and becomes a universal source of light and genial attraction. The very existence of neighbourly ties sanctifies intercourse. Never did Science before, thus re-echo, from the deeps of the sea, the hosannahs, which rang through the firmament at the birth of the Prince of Peace: "Glory to God in the highest; on earth peace, and good-will towards men."

As a specimen of the connection between the diffusion of intelligence and national peace, it may be stated that if there had been a telegraph, the last war with Great Britain might have been avoided. The British Orders in Council, which restricted our commerce on the continent, and which constituted one of the prominent causes of our Declaration of War in 1812, were actually repealed before that declaration was made, although the slow rate, at which intelligence then travelled, prevented our receipt of the intelligence in time. So also the great battle of New Orleans was fought after the preliminaries of peace were signed; but there was no telegraph to flash an armistice into the smoke of the contending armies.

In proportion as the nations are brought into daily communication, mutual respect and sympathy are engendered. Diplomacy will cease to be a mischievous appendage to thrones and cabinets. And since no movement can occur in national policy without its instantaneous communication to the whole world, it is clear that the Telegraph must become the Oracle of Peace. Congruous to its character, is its first enunciation of peace with China, and intercourse established between the civilized world and three hundred millions of hitherto self-inclosed barbarians!

No two nations on the earth ought to be united by firmer bonds than those two, whose telegraphic stations now respond flash to flash. War between England and America would imperil the interests of civilization. Welcome to all Anglo-Saxon hearts is the new union-tie, which enables the Royal Queen and the Republican President to exchange, on the same day, mutual congratulations in behalf of fifty millions of kindred freemen. May the British lion and the American eagle ever dwell in peace together, and the little child of the telegraph lead them. In the eloquent language of GOVERNOR KING, of New York, at a recent celebration, "For England I have a noble, kindred feeling. In common she speaks the language of Shakspeare, Milton, Bacon, and Newton; and united, we may walk down the future centuries, a mutual benefit, and the hope of struggling nations."

2. Another benefit of the Atlantic Telegraph is in its *relations to commerce.* A merchant* justly remarked, in the New York Chamber of Commerce, of the newly-laid telegraph, "We hail this as a commercial enterprise, carried into effect, more than for any other purpose, to answer the demand of a growing commerce,—of a commerce guided by the light of an advancing civilization."

Intelligence aids commerce in many ways. First, it places the operations of commerce upon the true and broad foundation of knowledge. Secondly, it gives regularity to its laws. Thirdly, it stimulates its advances into all quarters of the globe. And Fourthly, it gives equality to all who engage in its enterprises.

A knowledge of the state of the markets in all parts of the world, at the time of acting, must effectually check rash and illegitimate speculation. The telegraphs in our own country have already equalized prices throughout its length and breadth, and regulated exchanges with the most exact precision. The same results will be now obtained for commercial operations between Great Britain and America, and eventually for the whole world. The quotations of the business of the day on the Royal Exchange and at the Bourse, whose transactions close an hour or two before those in Wall Street begin, will have a daily influence upon the American market. And soon, the Exchanges of all the capitals on both hemispheres being in full telegraphic and commercial union, Commerce will possess the advantage of a new power, worthy of the mysterious winds that waft her ships and of the grand seas that bear them in their course.

It is a remarkable fact that one of the earliest mercantile results of the Atlantic Telegraph was to communicate the information of renewed intercourse with China, thus placing American vessels, trading with that distant land, on the same footing with English or other foreign vessels, which otherwise would have had the start of ten or fifteen days.

The Atlantic Telegraph is to Commerce what the gathering of facts is to Science. It encourages, enlarges, purifies, invigorates and confirms its domain. Let Commerce, then, bring her offerings from afar, gather her tributes from every shore, and wherever the winds swell the glad sails of her ships, do homage to this new benefactor of the great mercantile world.

3. The advantages of the Telegraph to *the various branches of mechanical labour* are incalculable. Knowledge and civilization are the allies of human industry. Every new invention tends to mitigate human toil, to dignify labour, to increase the sources of comfort, and to elevate the working classes, intellectually, morally, and politically. The labourer with his barrow, the blacksmith at

* Mr. A. A. Low.

his forge, the boat-builder in his yard, the shoemaker with his last, the tinman at his instruments, the carpenter with his saw, the mason with his trowel, the hatter at his block, the painter with his brush, the printer at his types, the tailor with his needle, in short, all mechanics, of every occupation and grade,—and work is honourable in all; idleness is vice—I say, all mechanics are interested in, and benefited by, every discovery and invention of the age. It might have seemed to some a singular and incongruous thing, to see workingmen in New York turn out in a procession, two miles in length, on the day the success of the laying of the Atlantic cable was announced. With a full band of music and with banners, the hardy workmen, in their everyday clothes, marched in a festival procession, which extended from Union Square to the Park. This was the testimony of men of sense to the general value of the new improvement, and to its influence on their own interests and happiness. Whatever promotes the prosperity of the city and of the country, helps the cause of the labourer and the mechanic. This principle is as true as the hammer to the head of the nail, or a plummet dropping straight down by the side of a wall.

When the working men of New York had assembled in the Park, the President of the Commissioners of the Central Park thus forcibly addressed them.

"*Fellow-citizens and fellow-workmen of the Central Park:* This procession of labouring men of the city, turning spontaneously from their daily work into line of two miles long, with ploughs, drays, spades, and all the insignia of labour, adds a most significant feature to the celebration of this most wonderful achievement of time. While bankers, and brokers, and shipowners, and manufacturers are all fathoming the influence of this event upon their peculiar vocations, the intelligence of the labouring man is not behind in discovering its bearings upon his interests and the interests of labour throughout the world. Movement, activity, transportation by rail and by ship, by land and by sea, are the life of this great market-place of the West and of the East. All inventions facilitating the exchange of material products and articles, and the interchange of thought, must enhance the greatness of this metropolis; and it is not singular that you who are engaged in a work that is to add beauty to its greatness should sympathize in an event that so deeply concerns its advancement. Whatever tends to equalize the prices of commodities operates to arrest those sudden periodical shocks that paralyse trade and manufactures, and bear so heavily upon labour. This the ocean telegraph must do, and I find a chief gratification in a faith that points out to me this result. While officials speak of this event in the language of state, this demonstration of labour shows that the great heart of the people beats with an enthusiasm worthy of the day and of the wonder of ages. It cannot be that this new avenue of thought, that brings the civilized people of the earth within an hour of each other, will ever fail to subserve the highest interests of humanity."

4. The power of the telegraph in *extending the knowledge and influence of republican institutions* will aid to bless the world. Our country has remained isolated from the nations until the well-being of its free institutions has been well demonstrated in its history. The Old World has felt some of the movements of liberty; but its irregular fires of inspiration have been followed by desolation. Before the influence of America in overthrowing tyranny could be fully felt upon the earth, it was necessary to bring its system of government into closer proximity with the Old World. Steamships and the press have already contributed to this result; and now, the quick light of the telegraph exhibits, side by side, the institutions of freedom and the thrones of tyranny. The cause of liberty always gains by light. The increase of knowledge tends to the political regeneration of the earth and to the establishment of the great principles of popular government from pole to pole. "The tyrants of the world will quail under the searching glances of an argus-eyed public sentiment. The present system of telegraphing is, as it were, blending the mind of the world into one stupendous republic."

All inventions are in freedom's favour. It has been said that the locomotive was a great democrat; and so it is, in the true sense of that word. In the same enlarged signification, the Atlantic Telegraph is a true republican. Railways and electric wires unite in unfolding the glories of self-government to expectant nations; and even the interest, taken by Americans in the very celebration of the Atlantic Telegraph, goes up, like a jubilant shout, to cheer the hopes of the oppressed and to warn Tyranny of its doom. Soon may Freedom's be a universal dominion:

"And henceforth, there shall be no chain,
Save underneath the sea,
The wires shall murmur through the main
Sweet songs of liberty."

5. The influence of the telegraph upon *the press* will be salutary and powerful. More than any other department of business, the press feels the power of this great enterprise, which establishes almost instantaneous communication with all parts of the world. The Telegraph will not only stimulate the desire of the people for intelligence, but it will throw increased ability and activity into the press, in order to meet the growing demands of the public. The newspaper is one of the great institutions of the age. If its necessity has ever before been questioned, all doubt of its power and usefulness vanishes before the landward and seaward telegraphs, which send to the press the contributions of all nations.

6. *Science* shall receive rewards from her own achievements. The ocean telegraph has been already of use to science, by

showing what modifications the electric wave undergoes under such new circumstances. It will serve, if it endures, to throw light upon the velocity of galvanic electricity, and enable the electrician to investigate the general laws of the fluid, when thus constrained.

The Atlantic Telegraph can also be employed in determining the difference of longitude between observatories, or stations, in Europe and America, and may be brought into use for certain astronomical purposes.

It is, in short, a piece of philosophical apparatus on a grand scale. The electrician will cherish it with the love of the astronomer to his telescope, or the chemist to his retort. Its connection with further discoveries is a certainty in an age of physical inquiry.*

Among the rewards of science on this occasion, is the universal homage yielded by the multitude. No longer regarded as an aristocrat of high pretensions, living in the seclusion of a grand, but selfish and useless domain, Science is welcomed as the handmaid of industry and the arts, and obtains from the masses to-day the most triumphant honours. This restoration to her true position is proof of her native dignity and worth. Never has Science received so hearty and gracious a demonstration to her praise. Whilst Jupiter places at her feet the thunderbolts of the firmament, and Neptune the trident of the Ocean, and Vulcan the miraculous implements of Cyclopean forges, the crown of glory is placed upon her head by the Queen of Beauty, amidst acclamations which fill the conclave.

7. The benefits which the telegraph will confer upon the cause of *Religion*, are as certain as that Religion's is the greatest cause on earth. Christianity has, in the first place, a common interest in all that relates to the advancement of society. Whatever cultivates good-will among men, facilitates commerce, stimulates industry, enlarges the sphere of free institutions, benefits the press, and aids science and knowledge, advances religion too. Every new discovery is tributary to the kingdom of Christ. Of how much use to religion has been the telescope, the microscope, the compass, the loom, the printing-press, the steam-engine! Thus will it also be with the Atlantic Telegraph, through the general relation between the progress of society and the cause of truth and righteousness.

But further than this. Religion derives a direct advantage from

* The "London Morning Post" says, that it is understood that the Atlantic Cable *transmits* the electricity with sufficient rapidity, but that it *retains* it, time being required for its discharge, after it has been communicated to the wire. The first signal is transmitted instantaneously; but the wire does not readily part with the charge, and the electricity it retains prevents the effect of a second signal from being perceived on the distant instrument. This difficulty, which was experienced in the Telegraph to the Hague, was overcome by discharging the wire after each signal, and this was done by sending the electrical current in the reverse direction. Such an arrangement does not seem to be sufficient to put the Atlantic Cable in satisfactory working order. Science, however, will doubtless discover a remedy in due time.

the use of the telegraph, like the secular interests of society. A knowledge of the state of mankind in every nation constitutes the basis of evangelical effort, and stimulates the prayer and zeal requisite to carry on its operations. If the angels of heaven were to descend, as visible messengers, to report daily the condition of the world, they would perform the service that the telegraph, in the name of heaven's King, is commissioned to do, through the inspirations of its swift-winged words. Every agent on earth is God's agent to execute his will. The luminary that compasses the circuit of the heavens, and the time-defying spark that pervades the cable of the deep, have each, in their origin, purpose, and results, a relation to Deity. God carries forward the plan of redemption by means of the vast system of events, which, each and all, small and great, old and new, make up the glory of Providence. Telegraphs ride over mountains, and leap through the seas, that they may prepare the highway of the Lord, and be the forerunners of the chariots of his salvation.

It is easy to realize that this great invention of the century impresses upon the mind and heart of the religious world the idea of UNITY, and thus aids in creating a power, antagonistic to the injurious separations and alienations, too long prevalent in the Church. A better era is at hand. Unity is the familiar lesson among the religious demonstrations of Providence. Unity is the loving truth of Gospel grace. Unity springs from genuine Christian intercourse, like the morning light, to bless the world. Unity gladdens the train of enlarged evangelical efforts among the millions of mankind. Unity is celebrated by the moral influences of each world-related event. Unity is transmitted, with the love of God, to the Church, in every new memorial of His power and glory.

Such is a brief view of the general blessings radiating from this work of light, whose success we are met to celebrate.

It is not, indeed, to be disguised that the telegraph may also be employed for purposes of evil. If Satan transformed himself into an angel of light, it is no marvel if he still use the agency of light in strengthening his influence and dominion. But, for the purposes of the wicked, light is the most hazardous and self-destructive of all weapons. The devil, in his attempts to quote Scripture, was overwhelmed by the replies of the Son of Man. All assaults upon the cause of truth and liberty through the telegraph, will be repelled by the avenging power of right, in the Providence of the Most High.

IV. Another thought is transmitted through the Atlantic Telegraph, as a commemorative lesson to the immortal minds that celebrate its achievement. It is that this great event is among the most impressive, as well as the latest of the providential indications of THE APPROACH OF THE MILLENNIUM.

The age in which we live is intense with activity, change, and progress. There seems to be a marshalling of events to terminate a great and triumphant campaign. Behold the nations of Europe sighing after a better day amid the gloom of ancient systems, the Ottoman empire expiring in desolate impotence, the great and portentous commotions that have swept over India's plains, the Jews looking to Palestine with revived national aspirations, the unfolding of the gates of China to the intercourse of a long-excluded world, the grand preparations on the Pacific's shores, the opening of Central America as the highroad to the recovery of the kingdoms farther south, the numerous and industrious explorations in Africa, as if to connect her, in time, with the general movement of this electric age; and above all, behold the progress of Christianity in every land, and especially the existing revival of religion which is gilding the mountain tops, and breaking in with glory upon the darkness of thousands and ten thousands of human hearts;—all these, with other providential declarations in the political and religious world, announce a crisis in human history. The horoscope of Time points to great changes in the zodiac of nations; and all the events on this world of wonders seem to be propelling it towards a sublimer destiny. The kingdoms of the earth, as at the Advent of Christ, are in providential training, with a great expectation; and just at this period, the telegraphic achievement towards universal progress and unity startles continents into awe.

What is the consummation, foretold by this combination of uniform signs? It is no less than the MILLENNIUM—when the Lord shall reign King of nations as He is King of saints. This event, according to Prophecy, cannot now be far distant. Its exact period is, doubtless, beyond the computations of the human mind. Biblical scholars differ about the time of the commencement of the latter-day glory, mainly because they differ about the commencement of certain eras, spoken of by Daniel and John, in reference to the duration of the reign of Antichrist, whatever may be meant by that term. Many students of prophecy in the Protestant Church have fixed upon the year 1866 as the one that is to witness "the beginning of the end." Assuming the year 606 (the time when the Emperor Phocas conferred on Boniface III the title of Universal Bishop), as the year for the commencement of the persecution of the Church, they add to it the 1260 years, which mark the precise time of the reign of Antichrist, and thus arrive at the result of 1866, as an important era, preliminary to the Millennium, if not actually introductory to it. Some, however, reckon the 1260 years from the year 756, when the Emperor Pepin gave temporal dominion to the Universal Bishop, and thus fix the millennial epoch in the year 2016. Admitting this latter computation to be the most probable, the interval between 1866 and 2016 is not longer than might be expected, for putting into complete and successful operation all the means requisite for the full introduction of the Millennium; although God may bring it to pass at any period, like the sudden and universal illumination of the firmament by His messenger lightnings.

There can be little doubt that the millennial glory is to begin before many years. One of its antecedents is the preaching of the Gospel to every creature, a great spiritual work, which is in the course of victory. The prediction that in those days "many shall run to and fro, and knowledge be increased" is being remarkably fulfilled by the aspects of the times. The text places intercourse and knowledge in conjunction; just as the railway and the telegraph, which are the champions of each, and each of both, are usually found in juxtaposition. The telegraph will soon sway its amazing power in every realm; yea, it already reigns. "There is no speech, no language; their voice is not heard. Their line is gone out through all the earth, and their words to the end of the world." The quick, pervading nature of the telegraph is suited to a day of knowledge. Its cord harmonizes with the universal song, "Glory to God in the highest; and on earth peace, good-will toward men." Soon will it announce that nations have beaten "their swords into ploughshares and their spears into pruning-hooks," and that "the earth is filled with the knowledge of the glory of the Lord, as the waters cover the sea."

Nor is there any agent in nature that so well symbolizes the instantaneous transactions of the resurrection morn. "In a moment, in the twinkling of an eye, at the last trump; for the trumpet shall sound, and the dead shall be raised incorruptible, and we shall be changed." Amidst these scenes of miraculous transition, there shall be "NO MORE SEA," and "TIME SHALL BE NO LONGER."

Help us all, heavenly Father, to be prepared for these great events of immortality! And may our beloved land, with its banner of stars as an ensign among the nations, be among the foremost to promote the glory of the latter-day, and to utter with its telegraphs and its voices, "the kingdoms of this world have become the kingdoms of our Lord, and of his Christ; and he shall reign forever and ever!"

Appendix.

THE ATLANTIC CABLE.

SOME OF ITS STATISTICS AND INCIDENTS.

THE Atlantic Cable is one of the most beautiful productions of Science and Art. It consists of four parts. 1. *The central conducting wire* is a strand of seven wires of the purest copper. The strand is about the sixteenth of an inch in diameter, and is formed of one straightly drawn wire, with six others twisted round it. The object of this arrangement is security for the transmission of the electric fluid. Unless the whole seven wires break at the same place, the fluid can find its way through the cable.

2. Over the central wire, are *three coatings of gutta-percha*, which were applied at three intervals of time, in order to secure the efficiency of the work. Their object is to insulate the wire, so that it will transmit the electric fluid under water. The gutta-percha coating increased the diameter of the wire to three-eighths of an inch.

3. The gutta-percha is covered by a *five-thread rope yarn*, which was first immersed in a mixture of pitch, tar, oil, and tallow. The diameter of the wire was increased to nine-sixteenths of an inch, by this new covering.

4. Over the whole is *a covering of iron wires*, to strengthen and protect the cable. This exterior covering consists of wires, eighteen in number, of seven strands each. The strands are of the same diameter as the copper core, each consisting of seven wires. One hundred and twenty-six iron wires are, therefore, woven about the cable. The whole diameter of the cable is about three-quarters of an inch.

The weight of the cable is nearly one ton to the mile. Its cost was nearly $500 per mile; and the total cost was $1,258,250. The capital of the Atlantic Telegraph Company is now $2,000,000.

The latitude of Trinity Bay Station is 47° 50′, and that of Valentia 51° 55′. The starting-point in mid-ocean being 52° 09′, the course of the Niagara had to be four degrees south of west, whereas that of the Agamemnon was almost directly east.

The total *distance* run by the two vessels was 1695 nautical miles, of which the Niagara ran 882 miles, and the Agamemnon 813 miles, the latter having 69 miles less to run than the Niagara.

The total length of *cable laid* was 2023 nautical miles; of which the Niagara laid 1022 and the Agamemnon 1001 miles. The Niagara, therefore, did the work more economically than the Agamemnon, having lost by slack only 140 miles, whilst the Agamemnon lost 188 miles. If the Agamemnon had paid out the cable at the same rate with the Niagara, compared with the distance run, she would have sunk 942 miles instead of 1001 miles; or if the Niagara had paid out at the rate of the Agamemnon, she would have sunk 1085 miles instead of 1022.

The official Reports, published in the newspapers, state that the Niagara *anchored* at her place of destination, on Thursday morning, August 5th, at 2 o'clock, and the Agamemnon at 6 o'clock on the same morning. The difference of longitude between Trinity Bay and Valentia being 43 degrees, the difference of clock time is about 3 hours. So that the Niagara was one hour ahead of her companion, at the anchorage.

The Niagara *connected her end of the cable* with the telegraph at the Cyrus Station at 6·20 A. M., whilst the Agamemnon's end was not landed at Knightstown until 3 P. M., or five or six hours later.

There is a slight variation in the different Reports, made by the two vessels, in several particulars.

The whole work reflects the highest credit upon all engaged in it. In the language of Captain Hudson, "God was with them."

RELIGIOUS SERVICES AT THE STATION-HOUSE.

THE following is an interesting account of the Religious Services, held by Captain Hudson, at the Cyrus Station-House, in Newfoundland, immediately after the Atlantic Cable was brought into connection with the instruments. The account is taken from the *New York Herald*, of August 16th, 1858.

"On the arrival of the procession, the cable is brought up to the house, and the end placed in connection with the instrument. The deflection of the needle on the galvanometer gives incontrovertible evidence that the electrical condition of the cable is satisfactory. The question now is, how shall we properly celebrate the consummation of the great event? How, but by an acknowledgment to that Providence, without whose favour the enterprise must have ended in disaster and defeat. Every one feels that this is all that is necessary to make the celebration complete, and to mark the undertaking as the work of two great Christian nations. When, therefore, they all gathered together before the telegraph station they understood the purpose for which they were assembled. Captain Hudson took up his position on a pile of boards, the officers and men standing round amid shavings, stumps of trees, pieces of broken furniture, sheets of copper, telegraph batteries, little mounds of lime and mortar, branches of trees, huge boulders, and a long catalogue of other things equally incongruous.

"'We have,' said the Captain, 'just accomplished a work which has attracted the attention and enlisted the interest of the whole world. That work,' he continued, 'has been performed, not by ourselves; there has been an Almighty Hand over us and aiding us; and without the Divine assistance thus extended us, success was impossible. With this conviction firmly impressed upon our minds, it becomes our duty to acknowledge our indebtedness to that overruling Providence who holds the sea in the hollow of his hand. "Not unto us, O Lord, not unto us, but to thy name be all the glory." I hope the day will never come when, in all our works, we shall refuse to acknowledge the overruling hand of a Divine and Almighty Power. It is He who can rebuke the winds and calm the seas. He works in a mysterious way for his people. His path is on the mighty waters. We have seen His power in the tempest; and when we have called upon him in the time of trouble, He has heard our voice. And yet how ungrateful we are for all His favours, and how soon we forget Him when the trouble passes away like the summer cloud or the morning dew. On a solemn occasion like the present, we should feel more particularly our indebtedness to Him, and it is with a feeling of heartfelt gratitude we should acknowledge the many favours which He has bestowed upon us. There are none here, I am sure, whose hearts are not overflowing with feelings of the liveliest gratitude to Him, in view of the great work which has been accomplished through His permission, and who are not willing to join in a prayer of thanksgiving for its successful termination. I will therefore ask you to join me in the following prayer, which is the same, with a few necessary alterations, that was offered for the laying of the cable:

"'O Eternal Lord God, who alone spreadest out the heavens and rulest the raging of the sea, who hast compassed the waters with bounds till day and night come to an end, and whom the winds and the sea obey, look down in mercy, we beseech Thee, upon us, Thy servants, who now approach the throne of grace, and let our prayer ascend before Thee with acceptance. Thou hast commanded and encouraged us in all our ways to acknowledge Thee, and to commit our works to Thee; and thou hast graciously promised to direct our paths, and to prosper our handiwork. We desire now to thank Thee, believing that without Thy help and blessing nothing can prosper or succeed, and we desire humbly to commit all who have been engaged in this undertaking to Thy care, protection, and guidance. It has pleased Thee to enable us to complete what we have been led by Thy providence to undertake; that being begun and carried on in the spirit of prayer and in dependence upon Thee, it may tend to Thy glory, and to the good of all nations, by promoting the increase of unity, peace, and concord. May Thy hand of power and mercy be so acknowledged by all, that the language of every heart may be "Not unto us, O Lord, not unto us, but unto Thy name, give glory;" that so Thy name may be hallowed and magnified in us and by us. Thou hast controlled the winds and the sea by Thy almighty power, and granted us such favourable weather that we were enabled to lay the cable safely and effectually. Finally, we beseech Thee to implant within us a spirit of humility and childlike dependence upon Thee; and teach us to feel, as well as to say, "If the Lord will, we shall do this or that." Bless us, O Lord, and hear us in these our petitions, according to Thy gracious promise, for Jesus Christ's sake.'

"The 'Amen' which followed the conclusion of this prayer showed what a sincere response it received from the hearts of all present, and the depth of feeling it excited. 'You recollect,' proceeded the Captain, 'what our Saviour told his disciples, that if they had faith, even as a grain of mustard seed, they could move mountains. We have performed a work, or rather we are thankful to God for having performed a work for us, which has been ridiculed by a great many who regarded it as an impossibility. We have been peculiarly favoured in being permitted to be His agents, and we are pleased to acknowledge that it was through His instrumentality the work was performed.'"

www.ingramcontent.com/pod-product-compliance
Lightning Source LLC
LaVergne TN
LVHW011136110826
845150LV00008B/2373

* 9 7 8 1 4 1 8 1 9 4 6 3 5 *